CREATE YOUR OWN
PICTURES
COLORING BOOK

45 Fun-to-Finish Illustrations

ANNA POMASKA

DOVER PUBLICATIONS, INC.
New York

PUBLISHER'S NOTE

This book is no ordinary coloring book. It is a very special kind of coloring book, with 45 pictures that you not only color, you help create! Each picture has been purposely left unfinished by the artist. That way you can finish it yourself. A caption at the bottom of the page tells you what you must add to complete the picture. In many cases you can let your imagination determine a large portion of what you draw.

You will have the opportunity to fill the stage of a theater with an exciting scene, to design your own ship, to create your own comic strip, to decorate a teepee, to fill a haunted house with scary creatures, to show what a cat is dreaming—even to put yourself, your family, and your friends into some of these pictures!

Hint: Complete the drawings in pencil, at least at first. That way you can erase any mistakes and make sure the drawings look just as you want them to before you color them in.

Published in Canada by General Publishing Company, Ltd., 30 Lesmill Road, Don Mills, Toronto, Ontario.
Published in the United Kingdom by Constable and Company, Ltd.

Create Your Own Pictures Coloring Book: 45 Fun-to-Finish Illustrations is a new work, first published by Dover Publications, Inc., in 1984.

International Standard Book Number: 0-486-24614-0

Manufactured in the United States of America
Dover Publications, Inc., 31 East 2nd Street, Mineola, N.Y. 11501

The prince and princess are approaching the mouth of a magic cave. What do they see inside?

These children are delighted to see the wonderful kite that you have designed.

From a castle balcony these children are looking down on a lively parade. Whom and what do they see?

While Jack Frost strews snowflakes over the earth, you are having fun below. Put yourself in the picture, showing what you like to do in the snow.

Help Jack Frost paint a beautiful frosty design on this window.

It is opening night at the theater, and you are appearing on the great stage. Are you going to sing, dance, act, or perform in some other way? Show us how you will delight the audience.

Roger waves as he passes on the merry-go-round. What is he riding on?

The elves and fairies are visiting the magic tree. This tree will grow whatever you wish it to grow. What would you like to see growing on the magic tree?

The elves are going home for the night. What does their home look like? Help the elves by making a home for them.

Saturn, the moon, and the stars are very excited to see the amazing spaceship you have created to travel to remote planets.

Name of Planet:

_____

Name of Inhabitant:

_____

You have returned from a voyage to a distant planet. From memory, show how you greeted this inhabitant of that planet.

You have been asked to decorate the wall of this big building with a beautiful mural.

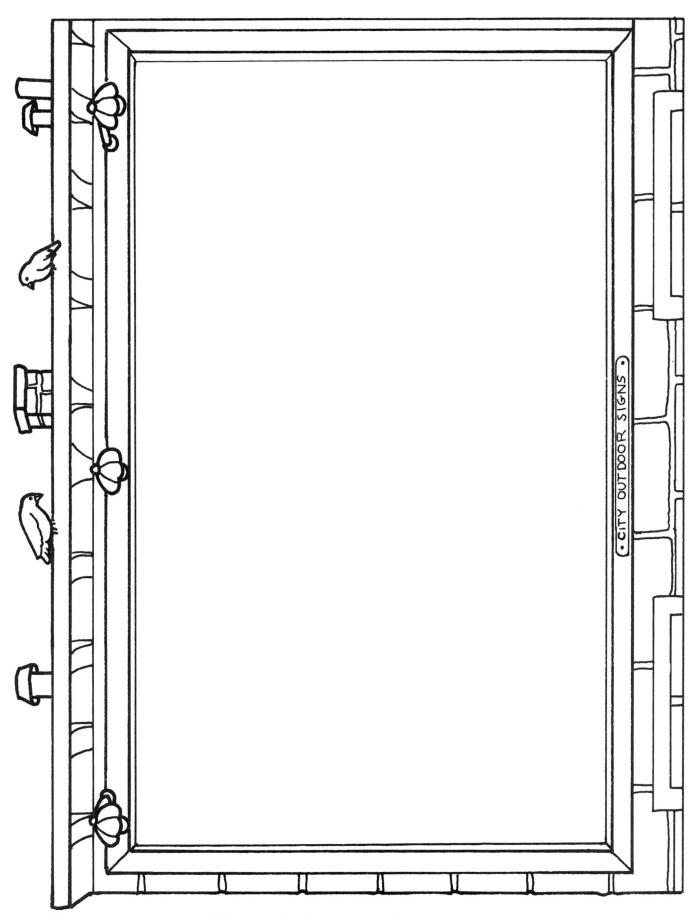

You have put up a billboard in the city. It has a very important message to communicate to everyone. *(Turn this page sideways.)*

Here are a couple of crazy creatures floating around the page. Draw some equally weird friends for them.

Finish the design on this page.

Here is a land with strange people and plants. Can you create some more people who are half animal and half human and who live on land or in trees, water, or air? Can you create some more odd plants, too?

If you could see music, how would it look? Draw the designs or pictures you think music would make, with the colors you imagine they would have.

Draw a picture of yourself as a superhero or superheroine. You possess special superpowers to bring peace and love to the Earth. Give yourself a name and a supercostume, too.

PICTURES OF MY

FAMILY AND FRIENDS

It is Halloween night. All the witches, ghosts, goblins, and other Halloween creatures are having a great time. Can you show what is happening inside the haunted house and in the nighttime sky?

Show yourself and your friends in Halloween costumes.

What are these young cowpokes looking at in the corral?

This teddy bear looks lonely on his toy shelf. Draw some other toys to keep teddy company.

If you were a frog living in a country pond, how would the world look to you?

If you were a flower, how would the world look to you?

Help these children create a very special sand castle.

Design a ship to sail the sea.

Draw the animals that live in this jungle. Some of the creatures you may want to draw are monkeys, elephants, snakes, parrots, and lions.

Create a mask for this member of an African tribe. See if you can make one that will have the power to attract good spirits.

What is this steam engine pulling? (Turn this page sideways.)

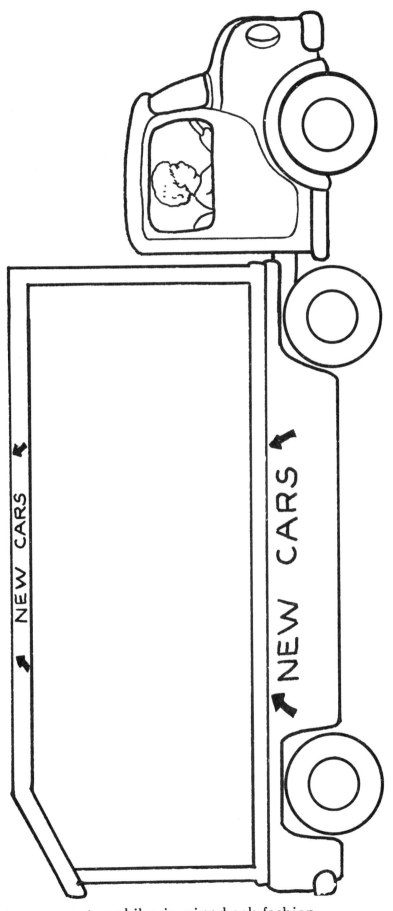

This special truck is designed to carry automobiles in piggyback fashion.
But where are all the new cars? Create some for the truck to carry.
(Turn this page sideways.)

You have just baked this batch of cookies in many different shapes. Now decorate them as creatively as you can.

Here are two more cookie shapes. Draw some more, and decorate all of them.

These children are excited about something they see in this shop window. What do they see? What kind of a shop is it? You can make it a bakery, toy shop, candy shop, pet store, grocery, bookstore, or any kind of shop you want it to be!

What is kitty dreaming about?

Will you help this Indian decorate the teepee with interesting designs?

Can you show us who lives in this castle?

If you were a mermaid or a merboy, what would you see in your underwater world?

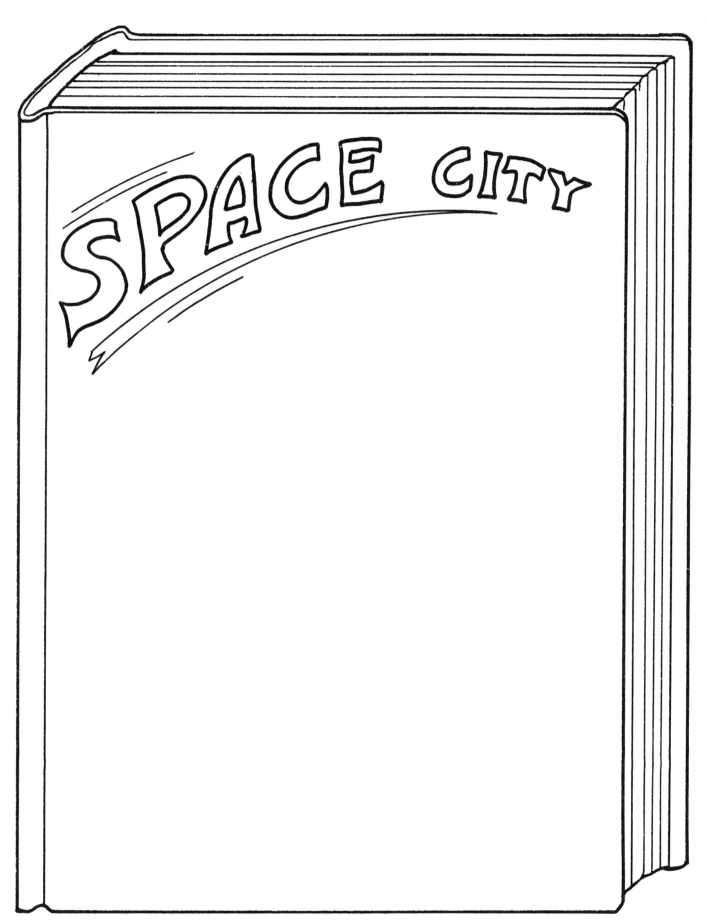

This book is about a city on another planet. Design a cover for it.

This clown is waiting for you to provide him or her with a face and perhaps some hair, ears, and a hat, too.

Create some puppets for the puppet show.

What are the children doing at the pond? Are they feeding ducks or fish, watching frogs or waterbabies, sailing boats, or doing something else?

You have created the most amazing flying machine in the world.

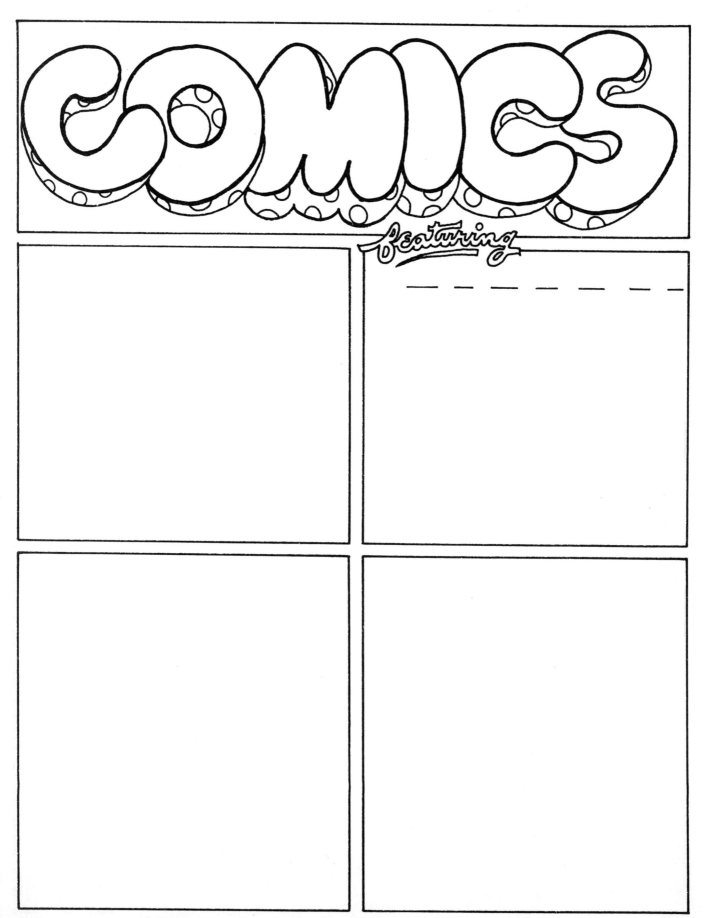

Create your own comic strip with your own character.

What do the children see on their balloon ride?